Find
In
Everyday Life

Latressa A. Crawford

Leah C. Campbell, Contributing Author

Copyright 2016 by Latressa A. Crawford

All rights reserved. No part of this book may be reproduced in any manner without written permission except in the case of brief quotations included in critical articles and reviews. For information, please contact the author.

Cover Design by Virtual Touch Printing

Editing by Dr. Pamela D. Thomas

ISBN-13: 978-1523921119
ISBN-10: 153921110

www.TheRealLatressa.me

Contents

Acknowledgements
Opening
Wink Wink..7
Red, Yellow, Black and White......................................9
Keep Calm..11
Needed..14
Left Not Right...17
I'm Talking About Me..19
Why Was I Created This Way.....................................22
How Dare You!...26
Cock-A-Roach..31
A "Special" Kind of Love..33
Second Shift..37
Bottom Line..42
Bottom Line 2..45
Ok...48
No Words...51
What Shall I Do...54
Tag Team..58
Christian Journey..62
Crossroads...65
Can't Even Die Right...68
Missing the Mark..71
Unloved... Loved..73
A Debt Paid...76
GPS..79
Obedience..82
What Are You Doing?...86
Something Happens...90
Ridiculous Victory..93
Atmosphere..96
Pride and the Ram..100
Bonus..103

ACKNOWLEDGEMENTS

I give Glory and Honor to My God and to My Lord and Savior. God knows that my road has been rough but I Trust Him that it is ALL for my Good. I Thank God for setting persons up in my life that I am able to write this book and share these experiences.

I thank Leah Campbell for her contributions, not only with writing but for the listening ear with many of these stories, "*You Know How We Do!*".

A special thank you to my editor, Dr. Pamela Thomas. You are a God-send.

I want to thank ALL of you who have Encouraged me. You All KNOW who you are (family & friends)... MUCH LOVE... I LOVE YOU MORE!

I give a special shout out to my baby, Christian. I hope that you will be proud of Mommy (Mom, since you have gotten older). Continue to trust in God and His plan for your life. Love You More Than Words Can Express.

OPENING

It can be difficult to find the joy in everyday life when life seems to be beating you up. Let me clarify "beating you up". It means it is difficult to find the joy in everyday life when your spouse isn't listening, when there is more of a 90/10 relationship with you giving the 90, when the school is calling in regards to your child's failing academics or when you are struggling with the educational system to get the services that your child so desperately needs. It is difficult to find the joy in everyday life when your boss is riding you about deadlines and you are closing down the building every night trying to meet all requirements and yet it is still not enough. It is difficult to find the joy in everyday life when your body is aching and possibly diseased. It is difficult to find the joy in life when you thought you would grow old gracefully; but your body has other plans, or when those hurting people you have helped turn around and hurt you.

But take heart, there is Joy in it All.

This book is intended to uplift you and awaken your subconscious into finding the joy and the lesson and or development in every situation that God chooses for you to encounter.

"You will show me the path that leads to life; your presence fills me with joy and brings me pleasure forever." Psalm 16:11

WINK WINK

I got out of the shower in all my glory looked in the mirror and WINKED at myself!

I had been feeling down about getting older, I guess you would say. Well, no let me digress. I was feeling down in the dumps about not growing old Gracefully. I had gained weight. My hair around the front edges had begun to turn gray, so much so that Ms. Clairol couldn't keep up. My once smooth and even skin tone now seemed blotchy. My creamy smooth thighs and buttocks now looked like a road map. I mean I didn't have all of these transformations until much later after I had my son. Not to mention, that those areas that were perky at one point were now heading south and flat lands were now rolling hills. This is NOT how I pictured myself at this stage in my life.

I had begun to feel very self-conscious. And with me being single there was no one at home to help boost my confidence. But one day as I was getting out of the shower, I stood in front of the mirror and proceeded to dry off and get dressed. I looked in the mirror and out of the blue WINKED At MYSELF! I was like "Did I Just Wink At Myself?!?" Yes, I did! Then the thought came to me, GOD DON'T MAKE NO JUNK!, which in turn brought to my remembrance the scripture "I Am Fearfully and Wonderfully Made."

Scripture(s):
For you created my inmost being; you knit me together in my mother's womb. I praise you because I am fearfully and wonderfully made; your works are wonderful, I know that full well. ~ Psalm 139:13-14 NIV

Prayer:
Lord, I Thank You for how you took the time to uniquely create me and to make me one of a kind. There is no one like me. Since I value all Your creations, that also means I value me because You thought out my unique design and took Your time into creating me. I will cherish this body You gave me. Thank You God. Amen.

Reflection:
Think of all that's right with your temple (body). Write down all of those things and then WINK at yourself for being wonderfully made.

_____

_____

_____

_____

_____

_____

RED, YELLOW, BLACK AND WHITE

Students: He's not Black!

Me: Yes, he is! Black people come in all shades.

Students: YEAH! AND COLORS TOO!

As a child, we sang the song, Jesus Loves Me and the verse that I loved was "Red and Yellow, Black and White, we are Precious in His Sight..." It just seemed to roll off my tongue and fill me with a peace. Even as an adult and while I'm writing this, I have a smile on my face and my shoulders are jumping. It's because I know I am Loved. God has no respect of person. He loves us **all** no matter what we've done and no matter the color of our skin. If God can love us in spite of, why can't we love ourselves or each other? Let us look past the outside appearance. What a wonderful world it would be!

Scripture(s):
"...Love your neighbor as yourself. There is no commandment greater than these." Mark 12:31 NIV

Prayer:
God make my heart young and fill it full of Love just as You did when I was a babe. May my Love not see color, race or creed. Lord, may I continue to have an appreciation and Love for All of Your creations. Amen.

Reflection:

I know that there are numerous times God has shown you undeserving love, however reflect on just one of those times. Then, think on how you are going to show that same forgiving love to your neighbor, brother, or sister.

_____

_____

_____

_____

_____

_____

Keep Calm

Testing is stressful for adults especially when your pay is dependent upon scores. In addition, you can imagine the anxiety of a child when their promotion to the next grade is dependent upon a single test score. Well, scratch all of that when it comes to this group of students; which caused *me* a **Great** deal of anxiety and stress. It really didn't faze them like that. However, I hyped up the test using mental trickery and it appeared they were finally getting an inkling of "I care just a little".

My students did not like the fact that I would not be administering the test to them and to ease their anxiety with that, I made small memos that I placed on each of their desks to let them know "I Believe in Them." No, I did not really believe in them; but I Believe in God and I had prayed, fasted, and called upon intercessors to join me. The memos said, "Keep Calm & I am Proud of You".

After testing, the students commented on how they loved the memos. I was glad that it gave them the love that they needed. It was such a shame that I had to turn around and spoil the moment with "constructive re-guidance". I mean my guidance went on for a good portion of the day. Towards the end of the day, I received a note from one of my students. I did not open the note at that moment but did so later. It read...

"Dear Ms. Crawford,
that note that you put on our desk it was nice But you need to Keep Calm. Keep everything good and nice. I would write 3 paragraphs for you. I like your lovely outfit, your ring, bow shirt, Bracelet, pants, earring.

Try taking three deep breaths. Try counting backwards slowly. Try Thinking calming thoughts. Talking to yourself.
Love,"

The child had become the teacher and the teacher had become the student. The techniques that the student listed were techniques that I had been trying to ingrain into the students (which I thought to no real avail). It let me know that the students were listening and what I was teaching was saturating their spirits. It also let me know that I ***needed*** to step back. The students were doing the best they could. They were eager to please me and wanted to please me. It let me know that I needed to let go and just let God… Step Back and watch the seed I planted grow.

Sometimes we can become so caught up in seeing the Miracle Grow, from a packet of seeds to a full-blossomed flower that we miss the fact the seed needed to be planted first and given the time to grow.

I took a picture of the letter and whenever I feel myself jumping ahead of the process, I scroll through my phone for the letter and read the advice the child gave to me.

Scripture(s):
"Train up a child in the way he should go; even when he is old he will not depart from it." ~ Proverbs 22:6

Prayer:
Lord, help me to continue to be a positive guide to those You have assigned to me. Show me Lord the right path to guide them along and to continue to plant seeds of life in their Spirit. I Thank You God. Amen.

Reflection:
Write down what it is you will do to offer *positive guidance* to the charges God has placed in your care.

_____

_____

_____

_____

_____

_____

Needed

"... maybe... they need you.."

One day as I was talking with my friend Anderson, more like complaining to my friend... The conversation went something like this...

Me: I need a change.

Anderson: What's the problem?

Me: My children are off the chain. I keep getting the children that are low and bad. I can deal with low but low **and** bad…?!? I hate to call children bad but... UGHH... I Just Can't!...

Anderson: Maybe God gave you those children because they need you.

That ended the conversation. That last statement by Anderson hit so close to home. It pierced my spirit and convicted me to the point that I had no comeback. Anyone who knows me knows that's saying something. When we are placed in difficult situations with difficult people, it is not always the change in us that is needed, but that you are sent to change the circumstances or the person or people. Your love is needed, that same love that Christ bestowed upon you. You are merely the vessel through which to transform your surroundings. Make yourself open and available. Let God continue to fill you with the strength that is needed to fulfill your assignment.

Scripture(s):
Love must be sincere. Hate what is evil; cling to what is good. Romans 12:9 NIV

Love is patient, love is kind. It does not envy, it does not boast, it is not proud. It does not dishonor others, it is not self-seeking, it is not easily angered, it keeps no record of wrongs. Love does not delight in evil but rejoices with the truth. It always protects, always trusts, always hopes, always perseveres. Love never fails. But where there are prophecies, they will cease; where there are tongues, they will be stilled; where there is knowledge, it will pass away. 1 Corinthians 13:4-6 NIV

Let us not lose heart in doing good, for in due time we will reap if we do not grow weary. Galatians 6:9 ASV

Prayer:
Heavenly Father, who has sent me to this place and positioned me in these circumstances for a reason; reveal to me my purpose at this appointed time. While I wait for Your revelation, I ask that You fill me up as I pour out to others. I pray for those difficult people with whom I must deal with. Continue to remind me that I wrestle not against flesh and blood, but the rulers of darkness. Show me how to reach them and help me to show them the same love and grace that You have bestowed upon me. Thank You for changing the atmosphere of this place, into one of peace and love. In Jesus name, I pray. Amen.

Reflection:

List people or situations that are a challenge to you. List alongside them what makes them a challenge and begin to pray for those persons and challenges, asking God to give you insight.

_____

_____

_____

_____

_____

_____

Left Not Right

LEFT, LEFT... ABORT ABORT...

As I was driving home at night, it was raining heavily. The roads were black and I could barely see the lines in the road (not to mention that my nighttime vision is really not the greatest). In an effort to adapt to the situation and meet my goal of getting to my destination, I decided to use the cars in front of me as my guide. The vehicles in front of me were the ONLY thing that I could see; no solid lines, dotted lines or solid dotted lines were visible to me. I began to follow the leader, if you will, but then I didn't like that term and decided it was a game of Guiding. Therefore, if the 18-wheeler veered right, I veered right. This went on for several miles. This caused me to become very tense because I began over thinking or trying to guess the forerunners next move. I gripped the steering wheel tightly, tensed up my body, and sat leaning forward trying to eyeball every move the vehicle made. After several more miles the truck veered right again and so did I. However, as I shifted to my right, I saw that we were exiting off the road to a weigh station. I quickly swerved over to the median, checked my left side mirror and darted back onto the interstate. It was time for me to find another guide. First thought, you cannot keep following everyone. There is your own path that you must take. Some people can guide you only so far until you must move on the path that God has for you. That truck had gone as far as it could, but it was not my destination. I was not to stop there but to go further. It was time for someone else to lead me higher.

God gives us earthly guides, people who He pairs us with to nurture and lead us. Pray earnestly about and for those persons who are leading you and take heed to the wisdom that they share.

Scripture(s):
Where there is no guidance the people fall, But in abundance of counselors there is victory.
Proverbs 11:14 NASB

Prayer:
Sovereign God, Thank You for sending the right people into my life at the right time to lead and guide me along this Christian journey. I thank and trust Your wisdom, the wisdom given to me and the wisdom You have given to those charged to guide me. May we forever, seek Your counsel in all that we do. Amen.

Reflection:
Who are you following? Who is guiding you and helping to keep you along your destined path?

_____

_____

_____

_____

_____

_____

I'm Talking About Me

As I was traveling down the road, I began to pray about a situation that involved myself. I needed clarity. I needed direction. As I was praying, the Holy Spirit filled the car. My prayer led to worship. In the midst of my worship, I **knew** without a shadow of a doubt God was going to speak to me, that God was going to give me direction. I could FEEL IT, and God DID speak but it had NOTHING to do my situation or me or the persons involved in the situation. God spoke to me about someone, well, not just one specific person but a couple of people. He gave me a Word for their Life. I was like "OKKKAY Lord". One person He led me to contact, the others He had me to be silent and not inform them. When I contacted that person, he was open & grateful for the Word. After I had finished doing what God had instructed me to do, I was like, Okay Lord, Me Next.... SILENCE... **crickets**... I worshiped some more and the Holy Spirit was still high in the car BUT there was NOT one Word for ME. God was Silent when it came to ME. Noooo, LORD, DON'T BE SILENT. SPEAK. I WAS PRAYING FOR ME IN THE BEGINNING. I DID WHAT YOU ASKED.... SILENCE...

Why would God be silent with me? I was thankful that He deemed me worthy of such knowledge in regards to others and that they received it openly. But Lord, I'M STANDING IN NEED. It came to me that by opening myself up to receive God's Word for others that in return

He was opening someone else's heart to receive a Word in regards to my life. Know that if God is speaking to you about others, then He is also speaking to others about you and may also have that person to be silent in regards to you. However, take comfort in the fact that intercession on your behalf is taking place.

Scripture(s):
But when the Spirit of truth comes, he will lead you into all truth. He will not speak his own words. He will speak only what he hears and will tell you what will happen in the future. The Spirit of truth will bring glory to me by telling you what he receives from me.
John 16:13-14 ERV

Prayer:
Lord, Thank You for deeming me worthy to be Your ambassador of hope and truth. Thank You for tilling the ground before I get there and making them receptive to receive a Word of hope. I Thank You that as I am interceding for others that You have placed persons to intercede for me. Amen.

Reflection:
Reflect on a time that you were in need of an answer or something more tangible and you received an unexpected confirmation.

_____

_____

_____

_____

_____

_____

Why Was I Created This Way?

Have you ever wondered why God made you, YOU? I have! I've asked God, "God why did you make me like this? I can get loud at times. I readily stand for justice when I see injustice in my presence and I often stand alone. I am helping even when I am mad or have been done wrong. My words aren't always so eloquent and the list goes on. *I felt* as though the qualities I possessed needed to be different to be one of God's servants and especially a servant who is in the forefront. *I felt* that my Spirit needed to be quieter and not so "enthusiastic". *I felt* that I needed to speak softer. *I felt* that I was too loud and boisterous to be a leader and that I needed to speak softer and meeker. *I felt* as though I did not speak of God enough, that I should be speaking of Him more. That I should be greeting everyone with "Blessed and Highly Favored" all the time. *I felt* that I was too bossy and commanding, that I needed to be *anything* BUT **That**!

God began to deal with me in regards to my question of "Why Did You Make Me This Way?". God began to bring to my mind various scriptures...

"Before I formed you in the womb I knew you, before you were born I set you apart; I appointed you as a prophet to the nations." Jeremiah 1:5 NIV

"For you created my inmost being; you knit me together in my mother's womb". Psalm 139 NIV

"For I know the plans I have for you, declares the Lord, plans to prosper you and not to harm you, plans to give you hope and a future". Jeremiah 29:11 NIV

God **knew** what He was doing when He gave me the qualities that He did. That He carefully chooses these qualities **JUST for ME**. God had a plan in mind when He created me. It says so in the scripture, "For I know the plans I have for you..." God **knew** that the qualities He placed in you would make you a valuable asset to the Kingdom of God. He **knew** that He **needed** those that would stand firm and declare boldly that He is Sovereign. He **knew** that He **needed** those who were soft spoken to whisper words of encouragement to those who stand out in the forefront. God **knew** that He **needed** those who spoke of His Goodness and of His Son's Saving Grace to sow seeds and He **knew** that He **needed** others to attend to those seeds.

Therefore, you see whatever deeming qualities God has placed within you He **KNEW** what He was doing. Those qualities are for **your good** and the **good** of the Kingdom of Heaven. You are a part of His Master Plan! You Are Needed and Valuable!

The enemy will try to discredit what God has placed in you and the purpose of your unique qualities. DO NOT LISTEN TO THE ENEMY. Know that you are unique, a custom-built model, made to handle Exactly What Has, What Is and What Will come your way. Before any negativity festers say this affirmation: "I am **YOU**-niquely created, **Custom Built**. I Can Handle This. I was

CREATED for This!". A custom-built model is one of a kind. It is tailored made to specifics. Be Who **YOU** are created to be!

Scripture(s):
"Before I formed you in the womb I knew you, before you were born I set you apart; I appointed you as a prophet to the nations." Jeremiah 1:5 NIV

"For you created my inmost being; you knit me together in my mother's womb". Psalm 139 NIV

"For I know the plans I have for you, declares the Lord, plans to prosper you and not to harm you, plans to give you hope and a future". Jeremiah 29:11 NIV

Prayer:
God I **THANK YOU** for making me, **ME**! I Thank You for the plan that You have for my life. I Thank You for how You oh so **carefully** formed me, instilling in me all the qualities that would make me a valuable asset to Your Kingdom. God I pray that You will perfect these qualities given me so that others may see Your Spirit in Me. I recognize that the enemy would have me to believe that what You have created is not good enough. But God I know because You live inside of me, because I am Your child and because Your Son died for my sins leaving me with Power; that in You and because of Your Son, Jesus the Christ, I am MORE Than Enough. Thank You God for making me Uniquely ME! Amen!

Reflection:

Write down all of your gifts and talents. How you are using them for the betterment of God's Kingdom. If you are not using all of the many gifts and talents given to you, then how will you begin to put into action what God has given to you?

_____

_____

_____

_____

_____

_____

How Dare You!

"...How dare you allow the enemy to steal from you all that God has put in you...."

These were the words spoken by my friend to me or should I say *texted* to me. God had taken me through something that I **begged** Him (I mean ***BEGGED***) for days on end to *not* allow happen to me again. As you probably suspected the "something" of course, was the hurt I felt by what another person had done. I was more so hurt by the way the person chose to handle the situation and that caused me to regress to a time of great pain. A time that occurred not so long before this current incident. I had prayed to God on the first incident that I never be placed in a situation like that again. That if I were placed in that situation, before it got too far... No! Stop! Even "before it got *too* far", God, RIGHT NOW REMOVE all persons and whatever it was inside of me that would lead me down that same path. Sure enough, God removed some people from my life. I was not sad at all, I knew I had prayed about it and they had to go. So, why did God after such desperation from me on the previous incident, allow this same situation to happen again. I know He knew the magnitude in which I had been broken. I didn't go to work for a week because I was so broken, not to mention the countless nights and days I cried. Yet here I stand, a broken vessel *again*. My whole personality changed. I didn't want to talk. I didn't want to come out of my home and I didn't.

I only left my home when necessary and then I made sure that *"necessary"* was far and in between. Soon came the holidays and I had to interact with people. I knew that I needed to prep myself mentally. I would look in the mirror and say "SHOW TIME", because that's what I was putting on, a show!

My friend and sister in Christ sent me a text to check on me. In this exchange, I began to release some of my frustration and hurt. Her next text stated…

"Latressa, this is not you! You are a fighter! How dare you allow the enemy to steal from you all that God has put in you…".

That struck a chord within me. One it made me realize how others took/take notice and that they in turn may be drawing strength from my strength. Secondly, it made me reflect on just how far I had come in the Kingdom. How God had grown my gifts. Yes, *gifts*, because I am Blessed to have more than one gift. Was I going to allow the enemy to have all that wrapped up in a bow?!? NOO! I had gone through too many trials and lessons. I had prospered spiritually and begun developing my God given gifts to another level/dimension. I had to pull myself up by the bootstraps.

What I had to do was put on the armor of God. There are times we must redress ourselves with God's armor. Though unintentional, the armor had fallen off with the onset of life's battles. Even if you can't pick yourself up, while lying down put on the armor of God one piece at a time, starting with the knee pads of prayer. Before long you will find yourself standing fully erect, adorned with your Spiritual armor and ready for battle once again.

Scripture(s):
In addition to all this, take up the shield of faith, with which you can extinguish all the flaming arrows of the evil one. Ephesians 6:16 NIV

Prayer:
Lord God, I Thank You for equipping me with the tools necessary to withstand the enemy. I Thank You for sending Your earthly angels to minister to me during my fallen time of battle. Continue God to make me strong that others may draw strength from me and continue to fight the good fight. It is all for Your Glory, by Your Might. In Jesus Name. Amen.

Reflection:

Write down all the times and ways the enemy has stolen what God has placed in you, all that you have earned through the overcoming of trials, all that you have cried for, and crucified your flesh for. Do you notice a pattern to his trickery? Is it occurring the same time every month, every year, with the same person or at the same place/location? How will you avoid this trap(s)?

_____

_____

_____

_____

_____

_____

Cock-a-Roach

Me: Complete the analogy, plants is to caterpillar as clothes is to…

Student: Cock-a-Roach!!!

How in the world did the student come up with the answer "Cock-a-Roach". I simply stood back in amazement and bewilderment with the expression on my face of "WHAT?!? HUH?!?". The correct answer was moth. A caterpillar, which is an insect, eats plants. A moth, which is also an insect, eats clothes. His experience was not associated with moths. It was associated with "Cock-a-Roaches". In trying to "broaden his horizon", it left him with a "WHAT?!? HUH?!?" expression on *his* face. The more I tried to explain the more frustrated we both became. I was like "MOTH. A MOTH... You should know this! What aren't you getting?". I had to then step back.

Judgmental means the act of judgment. Judgment is the forming of an opinion, estimate, notion, or conclusion, as from circumstances presented to the mind. Only after probing the student for more information did I realize his rationale (which by the way still did not make sense to me). However, what I learned from his explanation was that our experiences are not the same and therefore, our rationales/logic would not be as well. We so quickly judge others and take for granted their struggles and experiences. We assume that their struggles/experiences are like ours, when the truth of the matter is they *simply are not*! This assumption/judgment causes us to have frustration with others, in addition to intolerance and sometimes an indifference towards others.

I assumed that this student would know about moths versus roaches because of the area in which he lived. I judged that because of the area was middle class, he would be able to relate. I judged that the student would be knowledgeable and be able to grasp the concept after me merely just verbally explaining it to him. It was only after I stepped back, realized that his experience was different from mine, got rid of my frustration and took a different approach (which was to show him a picture) that he began to understand and relate. This broadened his knowledge, increased my level of tolerance, and decreased my assumptions.

Let us be less judgmental of others and more understanding. Let us realize that our struggles and experiences are different and let us explore different avenues of reaching one another.

Scripture(s):
Do not judge by appearances, but judge with right judgment." John 7:24 ESV

Prayer:
Father, Thank You for helping me to see beyond my natural eyes. Help me to see past the outward appearance so that I may meet the need of Your people. In Jesus Name. Amen.

Reflection:

Was there a time you were judgmental or made presumptions of others based on looks, social economics, race, where they lived, what they drove or their background? Did the presumptions help the relationship or help with growing them or you in Christ and or towards Christ?

_____

_____

_____

_____

_____

_____

A "Special" Kind of Love
By Leah Campbell

PREMATURITY, FEEDING TUBE, CEREBRAL PALSY, DEVELOPMENTAL DELAY ….Of course I was familiar with these terms. I had encountered them numerous times professionally in my experience as a pediatric speech language pathologist. I had worked with many disabled children who carried the heavy burden of one or more of these labels. These were not friendly, feel-good terms to bestow upon a child. However, seeing these words written and hearing these words spoken to describe MY CHILD hit me like a ton of bricks! "Lord, I know how to provide therapy with a child with special needs, but how do I parent a child with special needs?" "God, how did this happen?" This was not in my plans! I quickly learned that my plan for my life was very different from God's plan for my life. God had prepared a journey for me that would bend me, shape me, mold me but not break me. Little did I know this journey would ultimately teach me about a "special" kind of love.

The year 2006 was the year my life, as I knew it, changed forever. My second born son was born 10 weeks prematurely, weighing just 3 lbs., 2 oz. An older brother, who prayed for years for a baby brother, welcomed him. Immediately following his birth, our son was placed in the hospital's Neonatal Intensive Care Unit (NICU). Each week seemed to reveal a new challenge that had to be resolved before our son's health would be deemed stable enough for discharge. With God's grace, our son's health stabilized and he was discharged from the hospital after a 69-day stay. Boy, were we happy to have our entire family at home now. Little did I know this was just the beginning of the journey God had for me.

The first few months and ensuing years of our son's life were and still are very challenging. There have been many medical complications, doctor's visits, hospital stays, and therapy appointments. These medical and therapy appointments replaced play dates and social outings. However, in the midst of this drastic shift in priorities, our prayer life and family unit strengthened. We learned the true meaning of full reliance on God, the sustainer of life and strength. Nicholas is now 9 years old. Although he continues to face many challenges, his life has greatly enriched our family and his boundless energy, positive spirit, and winning smile have touched many people. Now, is this the life I envisioned for myself 10-15 years ago? NO, not at all! Have there been tears shed? Yes! Have there been days when I did not know if I had the physical strength and the mental fortitude to forge ahead? Yes! But without failure, it is during those moments of worry and anxiety that I am reminded that we serve a sovereign God who has a pre-ordained plan for each of our lives. We may not understand that plan, but we must learn to trust Him. I am learning to trust him no matter what the circumstances are. I once read that God is not committed to our comfort, he's committed to our character. Although there are times when I am uncomfortable, I realize that I can cast my care upon Him, for he cares for me.
(1 Peter5:7)

I thank God that he has entrusted me to parent my children. I thank God that he utilizes my children to teach me humility, empathy, patience and unselfish love. I thank God for showing me, His child, a "special" kind of love and allowing me to reflect that "special" kind of love to my children. The journey God has for me continues…

Scripture(s):
Your word is a lamp to my feet and a light to my path. Psalm 119:105

Prayer:
Father God, Thank you for blessing me with two wonderful children and thank you for being my provider and comforter as I travel this path called parenthood. Thank you for leading me on this journey. Please equip me to be the parent I need to be to raise God-fearing children. Nurture and cultivate them to become strong Christian soldiers. Lord, I ask that your WILL be done in their lives. Please bless and heal those families dealing with any special circumstances. Please help them to realize you are a Rock and comforter during the difficult times. I ask these things in your Son's name, Jesus Christ. AMEN.

Reflection:
How did this entry speak to you?

Second Shift
By Leah Campbell

I slowly pulled my car into the garage and released a long, deep sigh of relief...home at last! Still seated in my car, there is no radio blaring - no telephone conversation – no quick text message to a friend. There is just a moment of silent reflection and a quick prayer of thanks to God for the completion of another "first shift". For a number of years, I have jokingly referred to my various obligations and responsibilities within each typical day as either a part of my "first shift" or "second shift" responsibilities.
"First shift" duties include my professional work as a pediatric speech language pathologist with special needs students. I provide therapy services to children with a wide variety of communication difficulties. Although my professional job is challenging, it is also very rewarding. With all of its challenges, I would say my "first shift" is fairly manageable.

My "second shift", however, is that part of the day that is most demanding and requires the most prayer. It begins once the aforementioned long, deep sigh of relief is released and that prayer of thanks is concluded with an "AMEN". "Second shift" begins when I exit that parked car and shuffle my tired feet toward the door to my home. "Second shift" OFFICALLY begins when I turn the doorknob and enter the home I share with my husband and two sons. It is that time of the day when household responsibilities are front and center.

It is that time of day that ushers in a barrage of thoughts: "What will I cook for dinner?", "I need to pick up that prescription from the pharmacy", "Does my child need help with that project?", "Will I be able to go to the gym at any point today?" The list goes on and on. If I am not careful, "second shift" is also the time of day when anxiety slowly creeps in and attempts to grasp and consume my thoughts.

Anxiety will often lead us to lose sight of all the blessings God has bestowed upon us. Anxiety will cause us to feel inadequate, lose focus, and not seek God first to help us handle the responsibilities He has entrusted us with. We must always seek God's Word in scripture as a source of comfort when our demands are overwhelming. "And God is able to make all grace abound toward you, that you always having all sufficiency in all things, may have an abundance for every good work."

II Corinthians 9:8
God's grace gives us sufficiency in all things. As children of God, we must remember that there is refuge from anxiety and burdens in God. Rest and dwell in Him for continual renewal. "First, Second or even Third" shifts demands are NO match for our loving and merciful God who continuously stores and renews our strength. I pray that God helps me operate from a position of strength and not strain as I fulfill the role of wife, mother, daughter, friend, taxi driver, cheerleader, church servant, etc.

Scripture(s):
Be anxious for nothing, but in everything by prayer and supplication, with thanksgiving, let your requests be made known to God; And the peace of God, which surpasses all understanding, will guard your hearts and minds throughout Christ Jesus. *Philippians 4:6-7*

Prayer:
Lord, thank you for your grace and mercy. Thank you for providing your Word, a source of comfort to all. Whether feeling anxious, inadequate, or stressed, your Word offers refuge and renewal. Help me to concentrate on your strength and not my inadequacies when I feel overwhelmed. Thank you for using every situation in my life to shape me into the person you designed me to be. Help me reflect on your love and mercy as I carry out all of my day-to-day responsibilities. AMEN.

Reflection:

Are there times you feel pulled in many directions and wearing multiple hats? How will you now cope with those overwhelming feelings?

_____
_____
_____
_____
_____
_____

Bottom Line

Christian: I don't like John.

Me: Why don't you like John?

Christian: He's always looking on my paper.

Me: Well, don't say you don't like John. Say I don't like his ways. It's not him you don't like; you don't like what he does.

Christian: I DON'T LIKE HIS WAYS AND I DON'T LIKE JOHN!

My son, Christian, is a big part of my life. He has been a blessing but also a challenge. We are like yen and yang. For Christian, WHATEVER, comes up, comes OUT. He holds no punches no matter how hurtful it is. Often, he fails to understand why his comments have offended you. My mother and I have tried diligently to get him to use more tact, but as of this date, he has yet to change his ways.

Holding on to feelings can cause an undesirable eruption of rage or anger. Constantly pushing your feelings down is like throwing boulders into a volcano in hopes that it won't erupt. It is sure to explode and with the weight of the boulders more violently and forcefully.

There are times in our lives when we will need to be blunt and just lay it on the line. Times when we will need to say the bottom line is THIS. Jesus was honest and forthright in his dealing with others. Although he was straightforward, there was never any malice in His intent. When others know of your character and trust that your intentions are only to assist in a positive way, they are more adapt to listen to you. Let me add that tact **never** hurts. How you say or present things can make a world of difference. Use wisdom in deciding when to speak and when to be silent.

Scripture(s):
"If your brother sins against you, go and tell him his fault, between you and him alone. If he listens to you, you have gained your brother." Matthew 18:15 ESV

"And the Lord's servant must not be quarrelsome but must be kind to everyone, able to teach, not resentful." 2 Timothy 2:24 NIV

Do not be quickly provoked in your spirit, for anger resides in the laps of fools. Ecclesiastes 7:9 NIV

Prayer:
Lord, Thank You for being open and honest with me. Father, I Thank You for being a God I can come to openly and honestly. I know that You care for me and Your correction is for my good. Help me to be open with others for their uplifting and not for malice. Let my words be soothing and not of deceit or malice. Thank You God. Amen.

Reflection:

Are you harboring ill feelings towards someone at this time? How will you release these feelings in a Christian manner?

_____

_____

_____

_____

_____

_____

Bottom Line Part 2

Christian: I don't like John.

Me: Why don't you like John?

Christian: He's always looking on my paper.

Me: Well, don't say you don't like John. Say, I don't like his ways. It's not him you don't like; you don't like what he does.

Christian: I DON'T LIKE HIS WAYS AND I DON'T LIKE JOHN!

You've read this before in The Bottom Line Part 1 but this lesson is two-fold. In the conversation with my son I was trying to point out the fact that it's not so much John, the person, who really had offended him, but more so John's actions. I further informed him that the enemy, the devil, uses people. Sometimes the people are not even aware of their offensive behavior. They are simply pawns in an elaborate, yet simplistic scheme.

However, there are times that people **are** aware of what the enemy is doing and chooses to be used by him. Regardless, it's not the person that our battle is truly with, but it is with the enemy using that person. We must pray that spirit off of that person and pray for the right spirit to rise within us to deal with that person. The way that you handle and or deal with that person is ministering to the person's spirit.

It is breaking the chains of bondage over that person *and* developing your spiritual man. The spirit man is the God that lives within you, His Holy Spirit. The Spirit is fed and strengthened with each trial you overcome, each time you study His Word and with each prayer that you pray.

Scripture(s):
For our struggle is not against flesh and blood, but against the rulers, against the authorities, against the powers of this dark world and against the spiritual forces of evil in the heavenly realms. In addition to all this, take up the shield of faith, with which you can extinguish all the flaming arrows of the evil one. Ephesians 6:12 & 16 NIV

Prayer:
Lord God I Thank You for keeping my mind strong. I know that the battlefield is the mind. May my thoughts be pleasing to You and wrapped in Your Word. Help me to see past the human flesh of the person and recognize that he or she is being used by the enemy. May I say or do something that will help to loosen or break the bondage they are in. These things I ask in Your son Jesus' name and I do it All for the Glory of God. Amen.

Reflection:

Think about a time when someone offended you in some manner? Were you really mad at them or their action? What did you do? Did you handle the situation appropriately? If not, how can you better address the situation where you are ministering to them and developing your spirit man at the same time?

_____

_____

_____

_____

_____

_____

OK

There is a meme that shows a woman with "OK" written on her dress. However, on the left of her are the letters "Br" and on the right of her are the letters "ken". So, the bigger picture says BrOKen.

How many times has someone asked us how we are doing, only to respond "OK"? How many times have we asked someone else, how they are doing only to hear the response "OK"? This is deceit on both parts. Deceit on the person saying they are fine when they are not and feeling ashamed or as if no one cares to truly hear the truth. Deceit on the part of one who is asking, in that we don't really want to know how they are doing or we are too consumed with self, life, etc. to take a careful listen to the tone of voice, notice the facial expression or notice the watering of the eyes.

There is NO Shame in being broken or *feeling* broken. There are times when God has to break us to get the best out of us. There are times the enemy *attempts* to break us in hopes of separating us from God. However, **Nothing** can separate us from the love of God, His protection, His grace or His mercy.

Take Heart. tell God how broken you are. Yes, He does know, but He wants you to communicate with Him. He wants to heal you. He will send one of His soldiers to stand in the gap. God's soldiers are standing by ready and willing, listening for their next assignment. We ALL need that support.

Don't let the enemy make you think that it is only you. It's *not*. Being broken is only a temporary state and even in your brokenness you are still valued.

Remember:
Broken But Not Unrepairable
Broken But STILL Loved
Broken But STILL Useable
Broken But **Still Highly Favored!**

Broken is a *Temporary* State that lends itself to an *Elevated* State of **WHOLENESS**!

Scripture(s):
The righteous cry out, and the Lord hears them; he delivers them from all their troubles. The Lord is close to the brokenhearted and saves those who are crushed in spirit. The Lord will rescue his servants; no one who takes refuge in him will be condemned. Psalm 34:17-18, 22 NIV

Prayer:
Heavenly Father, I Thank You for being the potter. You are More than able to fit all the broken pieces of my life back together. I only need to give You every piece and surrender **every** area of my life to You. I do so today Lord. I thank You in advance for Wholeness. These things I ask in Jesus name. Amen.

Reflection:

Recall a time you have been broken but God still used you. Did you give him all of the pieces of your brokenness? Are you broken now? Write an affirmation on how you will give all the pieces to God. Repeat that affirmation anytime you begin to feel overwhelmed.

_____

_____

_____

_____

_____

_____

NO WORDS

Me: (Crying) WAHHHH!! WAAAAHHHH!...

There are times in our lives when things become so great and seem so unbearable. That is a sign that we have been strong for too long. We have not released. We are still trying to control everything. We have not fully given our troubles and our burdens over to God.

I can recall this one time when I was very burdened. Things weighed on me so heavily. I tried to praise my way through. I tried to call those things that are not into existence. All of which failed to the magnitude that I needed them to excel. Meaning that, they helped for the moment but only to a small degree. They more or less put a band-aid on my brokenness. I remember being in the shower with my gospel music playing, singing to Tasha Cobbs' "Put A Praise On It", "Overflow" and "This Is Freedom". I followed up with Israel & the New Breed with Yolanda Adams "How Awesome Is Our God" and Deitrick Haddon's "He's Able". In the midst of this playlist, I began to sob uncontrollably. I placed my arm against the shower wall, put my head on my arm and I WEPT. The weight of work, being a mother, helping others, being a good Christian soldier, trying to be financially stable, among other things had become such great a burden. I was worn physically, mentally and at that moment, I realized I was worn spiritually. I had not given these concerns over to God fully. I had not trusted God to handle these things in my life. *If* I had trusted God to handle them, then it was the fact that I did not believe that He was going to do it for *me*.

At one point during my weeping, I closed my eyes, threw my head back and raised my hand. I felt my hand being grasped and clutched. I **knew** without a shadow of a doubt, it was God. He had heard my cry, as He Always does. It was God comforting me. It was God reassuring me. It was God reminding me that He is an Ever-Present help in time of trouble, distress or grief. My tears did not immediately stop but the reason for my tears did. My tears now were one of gratitude. I am grateful for the fact that God cared enough to come through Heaven and space to earth and see *specifically* about me.

God cares for each of us the same. We are His creation and when you create something, do you not take the time to protect it until the time of its great unveiling? Of course, you do! God does the same. Don't be strong for so long that you weigh yourselves down... "Yourselves"?!? Yes! Your Physical Self, Mental Self and Spiritual Self. Give your cares, troubles, burdens and hardships over to God completely. One of my favorite songs is Tramaine Hawkins "Potter House". In the song are the lyrics "Give him the pieces of your broken life..." Give God **all** the pieces and allow Him to do what He does *best* and that is **BE GOD!**

Scripture(s):
"...I will never leave you nor forsake you..." Hebrews 13:5

Prayer:

Almighty God, Thank You for being with me in my time of need. Thank You for being an ever-present help in time of despair. God, I give You the pieces of my broken life. I give You my finances, my job, my loved ones, my spirit, myself. If there is anything Lord that hinders me from giving You all the pieces, remove it. I lay them willingly at your feet. You are the potter and I am the clay. Mold me God. Make me New Again. I ask these things in the Precious Name of Your Son, Jesus the Christ. Amen.

Reflection:

Think about a time you were burdened and feeling overwhelmed. How did God comfort you during this time?

_____

_____

_____

_____

_____

What Shall I Do?

What Shall I Do Lyrics:
What shall I do
What step should I take
What move should I make
Oh Lord, what shall I do

I'm going to wait
For an answer from You
I have nothing to lose
Oh Lord, I'm going to wait

I know You'll come through...
I had a long bout of despair and needed questions answered. However, it appeared God was silent on the matters concerning my heart and me. I felt alone and as though no one truly understood my pain. However, I didn't let my outside appearance show it. I only shared it with a small select few in my circle.

I often play instrumental jazz in my room. On this particular day, I was feeling heavier than usual, if you can imagine that, and played instrumental gospel jazz to feed my spirit. Someone came to my door to share some information with me. As I thanked them for the information and closed the door, I turned around and then I heard it. It made me stop dead in my tracks. The song "What Shall I Do" was playing but that's not what made me freeze. What caused me to cease was the fact that my entire class was humming the song. Not one was out of tune, off key or skipped a beat, as to what they were doing. They never looked up. They sounded like ONE HARMOUNIOUS VOICE. I **knew** without a shadow of a doubt that God was speaking. He had manifested Himself, His Spirit, in that room to speak to me.

The lyrics are
"What Shall I do, what steps shall I take, what move should I make, Oh Lord, what shall I do? I'm going to wait for an answer from You, I have nothing to lose, Oh Lord, I'm going to wait. I know You'll come through".

God had come through. It was confirmation that God had been hearing my aching heart and me. That HE was Still in control. I can't tell you that *all* of my burdens went away, but they were made lighter. I can also tell you that a deeper Praise went forth. I skipped my lunch, turned off the light and laid prostrate in the corner of my room worshiping Him.

Even when it appears as though God has not heard your cries because He is silent, don't believe the Hype! Don't believe what the enemy is trying to plant in your mind and don't believe the doubt that *We/Ourselves*, formulate. It isn't always the devil, sometimes it's *Us/Self*, that gets in the way. We can plant our own seeds of doubt, mistrust and unbelief. God ALWAYS hears His children. He **knows** each and every one of our cries, just as a mother knows the difference between the cries of her children. He's close at hand and **never** will He take His loving arms from around us. Wait on the Lord. He WILL Answer You.

Scripture(s):
"I waited patiently for the Lord; he turned to me and heard my cry. He lifted me out of the slimy pit, out of the mud and mire; he set my feet on a rock and gave me a firm place to stand. He put a new song in my mouth, a hymn of praise to our God..." Psalm 40:1-3 NIV

"Come to me, all you who are weary and burdened, and I will give you rest. Take my yoke upon you and learn from me, for I am gentle and humble in heart, and you will find rest for your souls. For my yoke is easy and my burden is light" Matthew 11:28-30 NIV

Prayer:
Father in Heaven I thank You for being close at hand to me. I thank You for never letting go of me. Even in my times of doubt You draw me closer still. Thank You for hearing every one of my groans, every whimper and every tear that falls. Thank You that even in the midst of silence You are answering my prayer. Amen.

Reflection:

Has there been a time God has spoken to you in an unconventional way? Did you take notice or did you dismiss it? List all of those miraculous signs.

_____

_____

_____

_____

_____

_____

Tag Team

Text: Do you think that we would let you get away that easy?

I had a car wreck and the woman who hit me lied and "loud talked" me. I know I know… How could she "loud talk" me? I was meek and mild. I told my story to the officer, which by the way the officer had to tell the woman to be quiet and let him do his job. Anyway, I told my story and the other woman got off scotch free and I got the citation. Again, I know what you are saying, "It's okay, the insurance would take care of your dents and hers." Au contraire mon cheri! I was having a difficult time paying for full coverage so I had to let it go. I know your next response… "Oooohhh!" I know your response because it was the response that I received from everyone I had informed with that tidbit of information. What made it even more discouraging was the fact I was getting ready the following week to trade in the vehicle for another vehicle. I was doing this in hopes this would lower my payments. So, recap... No full coverage, out of pocket expenses for my vehicle, citation issued to me and difficulty trading in a newly wrecked vehicle.

Let me express where my breakdown of faith occurred. After the officer arrived, I immediately sent a message to my support crew to pray for me. While waiting for the officer to make a decision, I said a prayer to myself and tried to look at the positives and the blessings. I said to myself, "Well, Latressa no one was hurt. Your car is drivable *thus far*. The damage seems to be mainly cosmetic and you've driven a beat-up car before, so what..." Then the officer came back and handed me the citation. I could see the smirk on that old liar's face (as to say Yeaahh, I Got Ya!). I took the citation, nodded, drove off and said to myself she won't prosper. I'm just going to let this play out as God would have it to play it out. My coworker, who was in the car, also began saying these things to me and my reply was "I Already Said that To Myself". The more I drove the **angrier** I became. I received a message from my supporters saying this and that and "praying for you..." I had reached my point. My reply to them as I came to the stop light was "STOP PRAYING"... "STOP PRAYING FOR ME"... "It was a WASTE of time to pray for me". Did I doubt what God could do? Nope! But I **Knew/Believed** in *my mind* He **wasn't** going to do it for Me. I stop responding to one of my supporters and removed myself from the group. I was *ANGRY*. I was *TIRED*. Life had become unbearable. Mishap after Mishap after Mishap had taken its toll on me. Even though I shut myself down mentally and spiritually, my supporters had not. They replied "NEVER" and "You told me and now I'm Telling You, COME OUT OF YOUR GRAVE CLOTHES". They sent prayers and added me *back* to the group. They TAG TEAMED ME!

They Tag Teamed me with prayers and inspirationals. They didn't give up on me. Their strength empowered me. I know this to be true because when I said I wasn't going to pray, I found myself doing just that. Not only that but prayer was also something that had become engrained not just ritualistically but engrained Spiritually.

It is important to have persons in your corner that will not only tell you the truth but also support you in that truth. This Christian journey requires that we connect with other Christians. Even Jesus had a support group. They were the twelve disciples. They walked with Him. They prayed with Him. They ministered with Him. Make no mistake that Jesus in all actuality *did not need* them because he was All God and All Man. However, He did this to demonstrate that WE as humans DO. He went through all the hardships, backlashes and temptations to show us that as we walk this earth; we too will encounter these things and need a support system. Don't fool yourself and say "I Don't Need Anybody but GOD!". Yes, God is all we need but recognize that God **also** works through others. Find your support!

Scripture(s):
"Walk with the wise and become wise, for a companion of fools suffers harm." Proverbs 13:20 NIV

"Two are better than one, because they have a good return for their labor. If either of them falls down, one can help the other up. But pity anyone who falls and has no one to help them up." Ecclesiastes 4:9-10 NIV

"A friend loves at all times, and a brother is born for a time of adversity." Proverbs 17:17 NIV

"As iron sharpens iron, so a friend sharpens a friend." Proverbs 27:17 NLT

Prayer:

Lord God, I Praise Your Name! I pray that You will continue to send the right persons in my life to support me in my Christian walk. Persons who will pray for me when I don't ask. Persons to encourage me, to push me, to enlighten me and to be truthful with me. Persons I can cry with, rejoice with and Praise Your Holy Name with. Persons who are not afraid to boldly come before your throne of grace on my behalf. God, I pray that I am that kind of support for someone else. THANK YOU FATHER! AMEN!

Reflection:

Who is your support system? Are they persons who will tell you the truth? Are they persons who will walk with you in the valley?

_____
_____
_____
_____
_____
_____

Christian Journey

Me: One of the BIGGEST mistakes that a Christian can tell a new fold is that **everything** is Sweet as a Christian. That the Christian journey is smooth sailing.

This Christian journey is not easy. It is not all smooth sailing, not every crooked place is made instantly straight. As a matter of fact, the Christian journey is a **Hard** one, full of trials, tribulations, pruning and learned lessons. Some may say that this sentiment is very discouraging to those coming into the fold. Discouraging or not it is true! New Christians need to know the Good, the Bad and the Better. New Christians need to know this and consequently those who've been in the fold for a length of time need to be reminded of this. The word Christian means to be a follower of Christ. Christ endured many trials and hardships and even pruning to prepare Himself for the great and ultimate sacrifice. So, as followers of Christ, we too must endure the same trials. What trials and troubles? Trials and Troubles include but are not limited to, being talked about, betrayal, hurt, loneliness, etc.

Now that we've got the "Bad" out of the way, let's discuss the "Good and Better". Take heart, though we as Christians *must* go through, on the other side of through is Victory. Just as Christ endured all of those unpleasant things, He had Victory. Therefore, as followers of Christ that means we follow Him into Victory as well. You have the guarantee that no matter what the situation, **YOU WILL BE VICTORIOUS!** There is an insurance plan when you join the Body of Christ. The plan is stated in Psalms 91. In this scripture, you are covered for shelter, protection, safety, 24 hour rescue service, fearless days and nights and body guard protection (angels); just to name a few. The policy (scripture) further states, "no evil will conquer you", which means Victory.

Who Doesn't Want to Be A Part of a Winning Team?

Scripture(s):
"My comfort in my suffering is this: Your promise preserves my life." Psalm 119:50 NIV

"It was good for me to be afflicted so that I might learn your decrees." Psalm 119:71 NIV

"For the LORD your God is the one who goes with you to fight for you against your enemies to give you victory." Deuteronomy 20:4 NIV

"Now this I know: The LORD gives victory to his anointed. He answers him from his heavenly sanctuary with the victorious power of his right hand." Psalms 20:6 NIV

"for everyone born of God overcomes the world. This is the victory that has overcome the world, even our faith." John 5:4 NIV

Prayer:
God I want to thank you for your sacrifice of giving up Your only son and I thank my Savior for His willingness to give His life for me. I understand that the Christian journey is difficult but I ask that you remove self and flesh and help me to see with my Spiritual Eye and Believe Beyond Doubt that *ALL* Things Are Working for My Good. Believing that I Will and Shall be Victorious no matter what the circumstances.

Reflection:
How will you begin to believe beyond doubt when trials come into your life?

_____

_____

_____

_____

_____

_____

Crossroads

Homeless Man: Question... What does God look like?

During Bible Study, at one of the service ministries, one of the homeless guys asked, "What does God look like?" This is undoubtedly a question that many have asked and or are asking and some may even make it a focal point of Christianity. One of the Deacons, who was there, responded "God looks like you. The Bible tells us that we are made in His image". I believe this statement to be true but want to take that a bit further. Geographically, people of that region (now known as the Middle East) were of a darker hue before the mixing of races occurred. Some would dispute this but it's fact that persons who live in hotter regions have very pigmented skin to adapt to the hotter climate. However, that is not the point I want to make. God looks like you and me. God looks like you and me because He lives within us. He blew the breath of life into us. God is life and therefore lives in us. His spirit is living within us. How much of God others see in us is dependent upon **us**. How much of God you see in yourself is dependent upon *you*. Your Spirit has to be fed. The more you feed your Spirit man the more others see God in you and the more you see God within yourself. How do you feed the Spirit man? How do you make that man Fat and Full? By Reading God's Word... By Studying God's Word... By Praying and having an Intimate Relationship with God. You are a representative of God. The lost are searching and watching and wondering what does God look like. Show them that God looks like you and me because God is Living on the inside of us.

Now in reading His Word it also means *applying* the Word. Others can see God when you feed those that are hungry. This doesn't necessarily mean that you have to serve at a homeless shelter. Feeding your neighbor whom you know has their electricity disconnected or is struggling, would be a manifestation of the God in you. It means clothing the naked by donating your very **gently** used clothing. Let me pause here. Don't give those things that are greatly faded, has holes the size of a fist, tattered and severely worn to those less fortunate. You know that you wouldn't want those type of items handed down to you. These are just some examples. The more you develop that intimacy with God, He will reveal to you exactly how to display Him to others.

Scripture(s):
"God is spirit, and those who worship him must worship in spirit and truth." John 4:24 NIV

Prayer:
God, help me to develop my intimacy with you. Help me to love others as you have loved me. For the Glory of your Kingdom, help me to display on a daily basis Your loving Spirit, that others may be drawn to know You for themselves. Amen.

Reflection:
How are you showing others what God looks like?

_____

_____

_____

_____

_____

_____

Can't Even Die Right

Text: I just want my life to be over!

Me: Don't say that! It'll get better.

Text: How are you feeling today?

Text: I Can't Even Die RIGHT!

Life for my friend had gotten overwhelming, almost unbearable. Actually in her eyes it was unbearable, so much so that she wanted to end it (the suffering she was feeling in this world). She explained how she had taken a few pills that were intended to make her sleep. She said usually two pills would knock her out and decided to take just a few extra. She took enough where she thought the job would get done but not an excessive amount. It could not look like a suicide. This was done in the interest of her family, so that they would receive the insurance money. However, this time the pills had the opposite effect. The pills allowed her to sleep for approximately 30 minutes. She was awake for the rest of the evening and early morning. Continuing her story, she explained how she tossed and turned *Trying* to make herself go to sleep but couldn't. In conclusion she stated, "Finally around 3AM I cried out 'WELL DAMN! I CAN'T EVEN DIE RIGHT!'". I informed her that it wasn't her time to depart this earth. That God had Greater for her in this Life. We were created for a purpose and He creates with an end result in mind.

Even when we don't want to be kept, God is keeping us. He won't let His Anointed go.

Scripture(s):
"So do not fear, for I am with you; do not be dismayed, for I am your God. I will strengthen you and help you; I will uphold you with my righteous right hand."
Isaiah 41:10 NIV

"I have told you these things, so that in me you may have peace. In this world you will have trouble. But take heart! I have overcome the world." John 16:33 NIV

For I know the plans I have for you," declares the LORD, "plans to prosper you and not to harm you, plans to give you hope and a future. Jeremiah 29:11 NIV

Prayer:
Father, I Thank You for sparing my life. I realize that there is a greater purpose you have for me. I pray that you will continue to order my steps in the path that you have deemed for me. Thank you Father for your unfailing love. A love that is ever present in my time of trouble. A love where that even though I may have given up on myself, Your Love Never does. Help me to display that same love to others. Amen

Reflection:

Why do you think God created you? What do you think is your purpose in life? Do you know what that purpose is? If not ask God.

Missing the Mark

Students: BOY! Ms. Crawford you sure are in a rush today!

As the morning began, I began going about with my daily tasks. In the midst of giving the students the run down for the day, they exclaimed, "BOY! Ms. Crawford you sure are in a rush today!" It was true. When I stopped to listen to the statement that they made, I felt my chest pounding and noticed my heart was racing. As I was going about doing my chores of the job, I never noticed that these things were happening to me. I stopped, took a deep breath and slowed down my stride.

So often, we are busy going about with our daily routine and or chores of life that we miss the mark. What's the mark, you ask? The mark can be several things. The mark can be enjoying life, enjoying others, or even the voice of God.

Scripture(s):
Cast all your anxiety on him because he cares for you.
1 Peter 5:7 ESV

Lord, make me to know my end and [to appreciate] the measure of my days- what it is; let me know and realize how frail I am [how transient is my stay here].
Psalms 39:4 AMP

Prayer:

Loving God, I adore and honor You. Thank You for breathing the breath of life into me. Help me to not be so busy that I forget to breathe. I want to take in the glory of all your creation and lavish in your bestowed blessings. Thank You Lord for life. Amen.

Reflection:

Ponder on a time you were so busy that you forgot to breathe. How will you make it a point not to get so caught up that you forget to smell the roses or take in the blessings of life?

_____
_____
_____
_____
_____
_____

Unloved... Loved

"...I'm in love with someone else ... starting something will not happen for us..."

This text came from someone I had been knowing for over 20 years and dated for a brief period of time in my younger years. Throughout the years we had remained good friends, keeping in contact and going out on occasional dates. I felt we had established a close bond of friendship and love. However, reading this text made me feel inadequate and unloved. Not to mention ashamed. Some of the things that came before and in the middle of the statement were harsh. Rejection is always hard but the tone of the text was cold, unfeeling and uncaring. I mean, how could you be so frigid towards me after 20 plus years of friendship? Yes, the rejection hurt, be as it may, it was more of the unfeeling uncaring way in which he approached the situation. In years past, we had numerous arguments and disagreements. Never the less, my mind failed to recall any that came close to the hurt that I felt with this. I understand you can't help but love who you love. I mean after all the heart wants what and who it wants.

I cried and I cried. I made myself sick with severe migraines for two days. As I lay in the bed praying to God for comfort, the words "God Loves You" rang in my ears. After a while I began to say aloud, "God loves me". Then with a little more emphasis, "God Loves Me". The next with a little more boldness, "God **LOVES** Me". Finally with conviction, "**GOD LOVES ME!**" I had to let those words saturate my spirit. I realized that when man says he doesn't love you, for whatever reason, God does for *ALL* the Right reasons. Despite outside appearances or defects in personality, God felt you were to die for. So much so, that He sent His ONLY son to die for us. How much more of adoration and devotion do you need? How much more can a love be proven? No matter what, **remember** that **God Loves You**. Tell yourself that when man (or even a woman) proclaims to you that they don't. It's okay, there is someone Greater that does **Love** you!

Scripture(s):
The second is this: 'Love your neighbor as yourself'. There is no commandment greater than these.
Mark 12:31 NIV

Love is patient, love is kind. It does not envy, it does not boast, it is not proud. It does not dishonor others, it is not self-seeking, it is not easily angered, it keeps no record of wrongs. Love does not delight in evil but rejoices with the truth. It always protects, always trusts, always hopes, always perseveres. Love never fails.
1Corinthians 13:4-8 NIV

Be completely humble and gentle; be patient, bearing with one another in love. Ephesians 4:2 NIV

For God so loved the world that he gave his one and only Son, that whoever believes in him shall not perish but have eternal life. John 3:16 NIV

Prayer:
Father, I thank you for loving me even when it feels as though no one else does. I thank You for loving me with all of my physical defects and personality faults. Your Word says that You loved me so much that You gave Your only Son for me. Help me to love others as You have loved me. Thank You for Your unfailing love. Amen.

Reflection:
Have there been times in your life that you have felt unloved? What caused this feeling? Was it someone else's words or actions or was it your own insecurity? How can you avoid and or combat this false (because you know that God Loves You) feeling?

_____

_____

_____

_____

_____

_____

A Debt Paid

Me: Hello, I'm calling about an account that I have with you.

Associate: Yes Ms. Crawford, I'm checking our database. I don't see you have an account.

Me: Well, I received the letter and the account number is… Has it been transferred to another company?

Associate: Ms. Crawford, I have tripled checked the account number and checked all areas of our database. What I'm saying to you is Your Debt Has Been Paid.

"Your Debt Has Been Paid!" Those words sent a chill through my body and made my Spirit leap. It was wonderful news that I no longer had a pending debt. However, those choice of words is what made me Praise God. *Your Debt Has Been Paid!* Why had the male associate chosen those words? Out of my numerous conversations with sales associates, debt collectors, customer service reps etc., I had ***never*** heard any of them use those words. My mother who also worked as a debt collector for a short period of time never heard those words and in telling her she became wide eyed. Your Debt Has Been Paid! God had not only taken care of my financial debt but he also paid my Spiritual debt. God saved my soul with the sacrifice of his son, Jesus Christ.

Your Debt Has Been Paid. Tears streamed down my face and I became so full of the Holy Spirit. God had intervened on my behalf without my solicitation. He knew what I stood in need of without utterance from me. Just like He knew our souls were in danger of eternal damnation and he intervened. ***Your Debt Has Been Paid***! To this day those words ring in my ear and Spirit quite often. It serves as a constant reminder to me of His Goodness.

YOUR DEBT HAS BEEN PAID!

Scripture(s):
"Christ suffered for our sins once for all time. He never sinned, but he died for sinners to bring you safely home to God. He suffered physical death, but he was raised to life in the Spirit." 1 Peter 3:18 NLT

"For by grace you have been saved through faith. And this is not your own doing; it is the gift of God, not a result of works, so that no one may boast."
Ephesians 2:8 – 9 ESV

"For God so loved the world that he gave his one and only Son, that whoever believes in him shall not perish but have eternal life." John 3:16 NIV

"For God did not send his Son into the world to condemn the world, but to save the world through him."
John 3:17 NIV

Prayer:

God I am So Thankful for You Paying My DEBT. I thank You for the sacrifice of Your son, Jesus the Christ. I thank You for Your son being a willing sacrifice, paying a price that he did not owe. You are the Lover of my soul. Thank you Jesus! Amen.

Reflection:

How do you feel with the words "Your Debt Has Been Paid"? What are your feelings about how God sacrificed the Lamb for your sins?

_____

_____

_____

_____

_____

_____

GPS

GPS: In 400 hundred feet, turn right onto Denson Street

Me: What's next? I wish you would tell me where I need to go next!

GPS: Turn left now.

I love my GPS and wonder how I ever got anywhere without it! I call my GPS "She" because it is a female voice that directs me. Once I enter my coordinates, *She* calculates my route and I in turn look at the listed directions/the turn-by-turn directions. I want to know every turn before I begin and then use her as a backup. One particular day as I was driving, I was unable to look at the turn-by-turn directions. I had to rely on her directing me step by step upon her terms when she deemed necessary to inform me. I began to complain and I said aloud "I wish you would tell me where I need to go next ahead of time!" Meaning that, I wanted all the steps ahead or at least two to three of those steps ahead of time. No, honestly, I wanted *all* the steps ahead of time. However, very shortly after that outburst the Holy Spirit dropped in my Spirit, "That's the same thing you want God to Do". It was **exactly** what I wanted God to do. It is **exactly** what *We* want God to do. We want God to give us all the directions ahead of time. We want to see all the twist and turns before we arrive at our final destination. We don't trust God enough to get us where it is we need to go. It is only when He reveals the entire game plan or at least gives us a peek into what is about to unfold that we place our trust in Him. However, the minute God decides that it's not in our best interest to know in advance and gives us those turn by turn instructions, we panic and become disgruntle and distrusting. We must learn to relax, trust God and enjoy the journey. There's no need to worry if God's signals have gotten crossed. They never get crossed. No need to worry if He got the wrong information and is taking you to the wrong destination. He knows perfectly well where you need to be and the best route to get you there. So, enjoy the route of the two lanes (just you alone), the HOV lane (sometimes He has others to journey part of the way with you), the traffic jam (those times He has us to stay right where we are for a season), the spaghetti junction (those times when things in our lives get chaotic), the pothole roads, the hills, and blind spots, etc. Learn to enjoy the journey. God is the **Best GPS** you could ever have.

Scripture(s):
"…Be strong and courageous. Do not be afraid; do not be discouraged, for the LORD your God will be with you wherever you go." Joshua 1:9 NIV

Trust in the Lord with all your heart; do not depend on your own understanding. Seek his will in all you do, and he will show you which path to take. Proverbs 3:5-6 NLT

Those who trust their own insight are foolish, but anyone who walks in wisdom is safe. Proverbs 28:26 NLT

Prayer:

Heavenly Father I Thank You for being omnipresent. You are able to be in the present and the future at the same time. You are able to see all of the bumps that I will encounter in life and know the best route for me to travel. God, Your Word tells me that You want only the best for my life; so much so that You gave Your only Son so that this may be possible. So today, Lord I trust You. Help me to enjoy the journey. Help me to listen to Your instructions and follow them without fail, even when I cannot see the outcome. Help me Lord to surrender totally to You and not to look to the left or the right but strictly focus on Your voice. Thank You for these things being done. Amen.

Reflection:

Think on various ways you can enjoy the journey. How will you enjoy those nasty storms or even those bumps in the road?

_____

_____

_____

_____

_____

_____

Obedience

"Give What You Have"

Me: I don't have anything.

Voice: Give What You Have

Me: I only have these coins.

Voice: Give What You Have

I sat in church singing and praising and in desperate need of a Word from God. Shortly the minister said "It's Offering Time..." I had nothing to give. I heard a voice that said "Give What You Have". I said in my mind "I don't have anything.". The voice stated again "Give What You Have". I began digging through my purse and only pulled out a handful of coins, mostly pennies. I said again in my mind "I don't have anything. This is *all* I have." The voice said "Give What You Have". Of course, you know the voice that I heard was the Holy Spirit speaking to me, commanding me.

I looked to the right and the persons on that side were placing $20 dollar bills into their envelope. I looked to the left and the person next to me was writing a check with a *few* zeros on the end. I felt so inadequate and my worth lowered. I began to dig in my purse profusely and finally found a few silver coins. At the end of scrounging, I had just a little over $2. I said 'Lord, this is all that I have but I give it to thee!" I left church feeling worthless. It was not because of anything anyone had done to me or said to me. It was simply because I had judged myself and compared myself to others.

Before the incident in church occurred, Christian had to have surgery. Of course, as you may already know, the insurance paid the minimal amount of the so many thousands of dollars owed. This was such a burden to me because I was trying desperately to become debt free and here another bill had manifested itself. Now, don't get me wrong the bill didn't compare to the health of my son but it was just one more thing added to my plate. As stated, I went to church and all of the previously specified events transpired. A couple of weeks later I called the hospital to make payment arrangements. I was informed that my bill was no longer in the thousands but was now only a little over $200. That amount was almost the exact amount of coins that I had placed in the offering basket. I began to inquire how, simply for the fact that I didn't want any surprise mistakes later. She said that they took a chance and returned the bill back to the insurance company and then sent it again back to the insurance company and each time they paid a little more. They did this until the insurance company said stop. I didn't need any more explanations.

My obedience had reaped for me a reward. If I had given into my own insecurities, I surely would not have had the blessing God had in waiting for me.

Scripture(s):
Give, and it will be given to you. Good measure, pressed down, shaken together, running over, will be put into your lap. For with the measure you use it will be measured back to you. Luke 6:38 ESV

And he sat down opposite the treasury and watched the people putting money into the offering box. Many rich people put in large sums. And a poor widow came and put in two small copper coins, which make a penny. And he called his disciples to him and said to them, "Truly, I say to you, this poor widow has put in more than all those who are contributing to the offering box. For they all contributed out of their abundance, but she out of her poverty has put in everything she had, all she had to live on." Mark 12:41-44 ESV

..."What is more pleasing to the LORD: your burnt offerings and sacrifices or your obedience to his voice? Listen! Obedience is better than sacrifice, and submission is better than offering the fat of rams."
1 Samuel 15:22 NLT

There you will bring your burnt offerings, your sacrifices, your tithes, your sacred offerings, your offerings to fulfill a vow, your voluntary offerings, and your offerings of the firstborn animals of your herds and flocks.
Deuteronomy 12:6 NLT

Each of you should give what you have decided in your heart to give, not reluctantly or under compulsion, for God loves a cheerful giver. 2 Corinthians 9:7 NIV

Prayer:

Father, I thank You for providing for me. I thank You for looking beyond my purse and seeing my heart. Your Word says that You love a cheerful giver. I pray that You continue to make me as such. May I continue to plant seeds to grow Your Kingdom and to know that this not only means monetary gifts but also time and talents. Amen.

Reflection:

Are you a cheerful giver? Has there been a time God required you to give when you only had the bare minimum? Reflect on a time(s) when God rewarded you for your obedience.

_____

_____

_____

_____

_____

_____

What Are You Doing?

"Anoint the walls."

I could feel death in that place. His presence was eminent. Now whether or not he was there for my cousin was different. As a matter of fact I knew beforehand that the angels were fighting on her behalf. How did I know? I knew because during my time of intercession for her, God pulled back the veil and allowed me to see the battle that was taking place. It was a battle for her soul.

We received a call that we should come to the hospital that it wasn't looking good for her. I called my prayer warriors and informed them and I myself began again to pray. As I was getting dressed I prayed. During this time, I was moved to take my anointing oil and I could see myself anointing the walls.

On the way to the hospital that same urge persisted. Upon arrival I could feel death's presence and the urge had become stronger. I began to lag behind my family as we walked to my cousin's room. The purpose for me lagging was to anoint the walls without them knowing. I swayed to the left and touched the wall saying, "Death Pass Over". I swayed to the right and anointed that wall saying, "Death Pass Over". I continued all the way down the corridor swaying back and forth, touching both sides and saying, "Death Pass Over" with each touch. My uncle finally looked back and inquired, "WHAT ARE YOU DOING?". I responded "Nothing". He shook his head and continued walking on. As he and the rest of the family continued so did I. I wanted to stop because it didn't look right but I couldn't, my loved one's life was at stake. The last of the double doors opened and my heart began to get weak but I knew that wasn't the time to be faint in my Spirit. We approached her room and in there was the rest of my family and their Pastor. However, my Spirit was once again urged to continue anointing. Secretly I anointed the glass wall and stated strongly in a whisper "Death Pass Over". You could see the greasy oily cross stain I had made on the glass and I wondered if anyone else could see it, as well.

We all exchanged pleasantries (for as much as we could for an occasion such this), their Pastor led us in prayer and they left leaving me there alone with my cousin. I sat in the chair beside her bed and figured, what could it hurt, I anointed her bed and said a silent prayer. Shortly after she woke and began to ask for her sister. I went to get her sister and they were pleasantly surprised asking "She's awake?". I said "Yeah". Little did I know that she had been "out of it" or as she likes to tell others about her ordeal "I didn't know I was in the World". I thought upon entering the room that she was only sleeping.

Inside I was **So Elated**! Not only because my cousin was now conscious and among the living; but, that I had been obedient to the unction of the Holy Spirit. What if I had not been obedient? What if I had worried about how things looked? What if I had been so overcome with my own fears, self-doubt and grief? Am I saying my prayer was the only prayer that pierced God's ears? That only my action of anointing is what brought her back? What I am saying is that I couldn't afford to take that chance. I had to be obedient. When there is something that you strongly desire from God and He gives you instructions that may take you out of your comfort zone, think is it better to be disobedient or obedient?

Scripture(s):

"What is more pleasing to the LORD: your burnt offerings and sacrifices or your obedience to his voice? Listen! Obedience is better than sacrifice, and submission is better than offering the fat of rams. 1 Samuel 15:22 NLT

Walk in obedience to all that the Lord your God has commanded you, so that you may live and prosper and prolong your days in the land that you will possess. Deuteronomy 5:33 NIV

We are witnesses of these things, and so is the Holy Spirit, whom God has given to those who obey him.
Acts 5:32 NIV

Am I now trying to win the approval of human beings, or of God? Or am I trying to please people? If I were still trying to please people, I would not be a servant of Christ. Galatians 1:10 NIV

Observe what the Lord your God requires: Walk in obedience to him, and keep his decrees and commands, his laws and regulations, as written in the Law of Moses. Do this so that you may prosper in all you do and wherever you go. 1 Kings 2:3 NIV

Blessed are all who fear the Lord, who walk in obedience to him. Psalm 128:1 NIV

Prayer:
God I thank You for guidance through the unction of the Holy Spirit. May my ears, eyes and spirit always be open and willing to Your commandments. Help me not to focus on what others may think or say but to know and trust Your voice completely. Amen.

Reflection:
Think on a time that God urged you to do something but you were hesitant or did not comply with His will. Was there a time you were disobedient because you were worried about what other people would say or how it would look to others? What was the outcome? How will you commit to be more obedient to His voice and direction?

_____

_____

_____

_____

_____

_____

Something Happens!

My Mom: I'm going to throw this bottle out under the sink.

Christian: DON'T THROW THAT AWAY! When My Mom Puts That On Me Something Happens!

My mom decided that she wanted to clean from under the sink and rearrange things. Well under the sink was a bottle of olive oil that had been prayed over and was now my anointing oil. I would often anoint my son and we would pray together. Though I had often wondered if he understood or even valued what was taking place, I wanted him to have the exposure of prayer being firsthand in his life for all situations. I wanted him to see firsthand his mother as an example of that. As my mom reached for the anointing oil to discard, Christian stopped her and proclaimed 'DON'T THROW THAT AWAY! When My Mom Puts That On Me Something Happens!" I was wonderfully surprised! Not only because he *did* realize the importance of the oil but also because all those times of anointing and praying, he was feeling the power! To God Be the Glory! It also served for me at that point as a reminder that even though I can't see how God is working, I've got to know and trust that His power ***is working***. The power is not in the oil because you can use Crisco, Wesson or peanut oil but if there is No Faith behind the oil there is No Power in the Anointing.

Scripture(s):
"He poured some of the anointing oil on Aaron's head and anointed him to consecrate him." Leviticus 8:12 NIV

No it is God who makes both us and you stand firm in Christ. He anointed us, set his seal of ownership on us, and put his Spirit in our hearts as a deposit."
2 Corinthians 1:21-22 NIV

God did extraordinary miracles through Paul, so that even handkerchiefs and aprons that had touched him were taken to the sick, and their illnesses were cured and the evil spirits left them. Acts 19:11-12 NIV

Prayer:
Heavenly Father, I thank You for Your Spirit and Power that is ever present. You are always watching over us. Thank You for being chosen as one of Your anointed. I thank You for the transformation that is occurring within me. I thank You for filling me with Your power and love. I believe what Your Word says about me. Help me to continue to Faith walk so that I may be an ambassador of Your Goodness. I Give You All the Glory Honor and Praise! Amen.

Reflection:
How did this entry speak to you?

_____

_____

_____

_____

_____

_____

Ridiculous Victory

Sargent: Your name doesn't pop up. There is no record of that case.

I had a car accident that resulted in me acquiring a ticket. I believed from the bottom of my heart and knew for a fact that I was not at fault. However, the officer chose to give me the ticket. I replayed the accident over and over in my mind. "*WHY*? Did the officer believe her and not me? Was it because I didn't rant and rave, like she did?". It wasn't just the fact that I got the ticket. It wasn't really the ticket. It was the fact that I had to go to *court*. In this particular county, regardless of whether you wanted to contest the ticket or just pay the fine, you ***must*** go to court. This brought up traumatizing memories for me. A few years ago, I had to go to court for a seat belt violation and failing to completely stop at a stop sign. It was no big deal for me to go to court. No Anxiety. I went with confidence and a sense of I am an American and this is part of the American justice system and Justice *will* prevail. OH-MY-GOSH! Some of the things that took place in the courtroom left me feeling like I was a serial killer on trial. I had vowed in my Scarlett O'Hara voice to NEVER come back to court again. I ***Begged*** God, "Lord PLEASE HELP ME TO NEVER COME BACK HERE AGAIN!".

Well look where I had to go back to, **court**. They wouldn't just let me pay the fine. Noooo… I *had* to be present and accounted for in court. So, in acquiring the necessary papers needed to wrap up with the insurance company, the insurance company called in regard to the fact that they had not yet to received the accident report. They had not been able to acquire it themselves. I told them that I had tried to do so via online but to no avail. I thought the report had gotten lost in the online system and decided I will acquire it personally versus electronic. I proceeded to call the traffic court division and they in turn informed me of my court date. I couldn't seem to make it past that because then my anxiety of going to court kicked in. I have never been one to give into fear and decided that I *must* face my fear by calling back (but at a later date). When I called back I was informed that wrong court date given to me by the previous clerk. However, the current clerk gave me a new date and stated to me that my fine would be over $300. Anxiety kicked in *again*.

A couple of weeks passed and I gathered my courage again to pursue acquiring the necessary documents. I prayed to God and said to Him, "*HOWEVER*, You Decide to Work This Out. It's Alright With Me. Give Me the Peace I Need to Proceed. I Accept It!". I drove around here and there and there and here to be told, there was nothing in the system for me and I needed to track down the officer who issued the citation. Huh?!? I'm Not in the system. Well, Lord where are you going with this? I called my insurance guy and updated him on what had transpired.

A few days later I contacted the police station where the officer was stationed. I gave the lady my name, citation number and the name of the officer. She said, "He's not here.". I asked was he gone for the day or just out and would be returning later. Her reply was "**NO! HE'S NOT HERE... HE'S NO LONGER WITH US**". All you could hear was my gasp. I was in total shock! The officer had quit within that short amount of time and in addition to that, had not filed my case!

When a situation *looks* impossible, know and trust that it is **not** *Impossible* to God! There is *only* the **Possible** with God. When a situation *looks* hopeless, know and trust that God has already worked that situation out. When a situation *looks* as though there is no way out, trust and know that God has a ram in the bush already waiting on you. *Is There Anything Too Hard For My God?!?* **N-O, NO!**

Scripture(s):
"I am the LORD, the God of all the peoples of the world. Is anything to hard for me?" Jeremiah 32:27 NLT

"Ah, Sovereign LORD, you have made the heavens and the earth by your great power and outstretched arm. Nothing is too hard for you." Jeremiah 32:17 NIV

Jesus replied, "What is impossible with man is possible with God". Luke 18:27 NIV

Is anything too difficult or wonderful for the [a] Lord?... Genesis 18:14 AMP

Prayer:
Father I Thank You for how You always have my best interest at heart. You know the ending before the beginning. I Thank You for your supernatural power moving even when I can't see it. I Thank You that the ending for me is always Victory. Amen

Reflection:
List the various times that victory seemed unlikely for you in the beginning but God gave you a Victorious ending.

_____

_____

_____

_____

_____

Atmosphere

Have you ever been disappointed? I mean disappointed because you had plans and God changed them. Plans for advancement and prosperity. Plans for the advancement of the kingdom and God changed them. Were you disappointed because the plans got changed or was your disappointment with God for changing your plans?

I was invited to speak at a well-attended event. In the beginning, I was nervous but gladly accepted the invite. I even prayed about what my topic should be, rather than immediately going with something familiar to me. As time passed I began to become less nervous and more excited. I began planning mentally for my presentation and even informed some people of my upcoming speaking engagement. Sometime later after my invite, I received a message changing the invite from speaker to helper. I was disappointed and very shortly the enemy began to plant seeds in my mind. He taunted me with his words and lies, "God didn't call you! This is confirmation!" and "Nobody wanted to hear you! You don't have a title on your name other than Ms.! And look at that, you still have Ms. and **not** Mrs.! You told those people you were speaking. They will think you are a liar." The statements were endless. These statements began to echo in my ear for what seemed like forever. I began to feel my spirit getting weak and then I remembered "be faithful over a few things".
You see, earlier that week and day I had made this declaration to God and placed it into the atmosphere. I collected myself and said, "Lord, I will be faithful over

whatever you have chosen to give me at this time and do it with enthusiasm." In saying that, I felt my Spirit begin to lift. So, I continued. "Lord, I will be the best hostess there is! I can still bless someone in whatever position you have set before me!" Suddenly it dawned on me that maybe this was a test. It was a test to see if I meant what I had proclaimed earlier that week and even that day. A test to see if God changed my status from big to small, would I still be faithful. There are times that we must be careful about what is placed in the atmosphere and released into the spiritual realm. After making my proclamation known to God again, I was restored to full power. I was excited about my new assignment.

Shortly thereafter, I was approached again and told I would now go back to my original assigned duty as speaker. It was clear to me that it was indeed a test of… Did I mean what I had stated? Was I going to praise Him despite the setback? Was I going to be cheerful and enthusiastic about my change in status?... I received so much joy in laughing at the devil. God allowed the enemy to try/test me, but I came through in the end. I was Victorious. All of God's children are Victorious in the end.

Scripture(s):
"The master was full of praise. 'Well done, my good and faithful servant. You have been faithful in handling this small amount, so now I will give you many more responsibilities. Let's celebrate together.'"
Matthew 25:21 NLT

For the word of God is alive and powerful. It is sharper than the sharpest two-edged sword, cutting between soul and spirit, between joint and marrow. It exposes our innermost thoughts and desires. Hebrews 4:12 NLT

The tongue has the power of life and death...
Proverbs 18:21 NIV

Prayer:
Father, I thank You for being so faithful to me. I thank You for trusting me with the small things and blessing me with things even greater. I trust You with whatever assignment You have deemed for me and I will do it with a glad heart. Help me to realize that every small opportunity is a greater opportunity to be a blessing and guide others towards Your goodness. Thank You Father for making me victorious in all that I do. I ask these things in Jesus' name. Amen.

Reflection:

Ponder upon a time you were tested. Did you pass or did you fail? If you did not pass that test, how will now pass the next? Create a plan for when the enemy comes to test what you released into the atmosphere.

_____

_____

_____

_____

_____

Pride and the Ram

Me: Sitting on the sidewalk thinking, "What Am I Going to Do?!?"

In my younger days, I made a deal with my mom that if I became campus queen I would stay on campus but if I did not become campus queen I would live off campus. Well I became the queen's attendant/one of the runners-up, which didn't pay for my board. My mother still wanted me to stay on campus and presented me with a list of pros for doing so. However, I was persistent about staying off campus. I would not let go of my desire. Fast forwarding, I did not find an apartment in time for school and did not inform my mother of my plight. I had no place to go the start of the school term. I was homeless and living out of my car. I managed for some time to fool many people. I did this by staying with some friends at their boarding home (known as "the house"). I would go visit and stay so late that they would say to me "Stay the night. It's too late to leave." Of course, I would graciously agree, all the while knowing that was the master plan. I alternated between "the house" and the guy that I was crushing on and or considered myself dating (I later realized it was a one-way street). There was a consistent game I would play with him. The game was that I would stay so late until he would make the offer for me to spend the night. I would at times pretend to be sleeping knowing he would not wake me.

I rode this merry-go-round until my friends at the boarding house said to me that I could not sleep there one particular night. I then went to my alternate, Raheen. Unfortunately, Raheen and I got into a huge argument that night. We often argued, but usually our arguments and sulking periods were over within a couple of hours. We would always resume our laughing and creating made up games. However, this night was different. The fight was more severe with him demanding that I leave. Of course, I wasn't going anywhere because I had no place to go. After much protesting on both parts, I stayed. In the early morning I left, as he had to go to work. Still fuming and trying to be dramatic, I left without taking a shower which meant that I would have to use the college gym showers. That wasn't so bad and wasn't my dilemma at the time. My problem was that it was early dusk and the college campus wasn't even open. This meant that I had to sleep in my car. I parked behind a gas station in an area that I was not familiar with but had what I felt, descent lightning. Admittedly, I was really afraid. I said a prayer that God would watch and protect me as I slept. I slept in the car for the next few hours.

When I awoke, I went through my plan of getting to school early and using the gym showers. I proceeded with my day as usual, attending all of my classes and acting as though nothing was wrong. The end of the day soon approached. Before I knew it, it was afternoon, late afternoon to be exact, after campus life had died down and all the persons I knew had retired for the evening. I was left sitting on the sidewalk wondering what am I going to do and where was I going. I sat on the curb wondering and praying. God answered my prayer. A girl that was in my art class drove up and began to ask me questions about where I was staying. I found it strange that this young woman was asking me such questions out of the blue. I finally had to let go of my pride and admit that I had no place to stay, that I was homeless. Upon hearing my confession, she offered her place to me. God had provided a ram in the bush. I barely spoke to this young lady other than exchanging pleasantries, yet she stopped and started asking questions about my housing situation. **Nobody But God!** She was *My* **Ram**.

My pride had caused me to be in an uncomfortable undesirable position. However, despite my hardheartedness and stubborn pride God *still* provided for me. Despite our sinful nature and disobedience, He *still* covers us, protects us and provides for us. *How Awesome Is God?!?*

Scripture(s):
Therefore do not be anxious, saying, 'What shall we eat?' or 'What shall we drink?' or 'What shall we wear?' For the Gentiles seek after all these things, and your heavenly Father knows that you need them all.
Matthew 6:31-32 ESV

And my God will supply every need of yours according to his riches in glory in Christ Jesus. Philippians 4:19 ESV

Prayer:

Awesome God, I want to Thank You for providing for me even through my disobedience. Thank You for forgiving me time and time again. Thank You for seeing beyond my faults and still providing for my needs. Thank You for always having a ram in the bush just for me. I Love You Lord! Amen.

Reflection:

Was there a time that pride caused you a fall but God was there to catch you? How will you deal with pride when you realize that it is detrimental to your spiritual growth?

_____

_____

_____

_____

_____

_____

Bonus

From the Upcoming Book "#ChristianChronicles"

Sleeping on the Couch

Note written by Christian: I made this for You. Get some Rest

We would often "make the couch up". This meant treating the couch like a bed and putting fresh bed linen on the couch. On this particular evening, I had come home and the couch was "made up". On the neatly made couch was a note that stated "I made this for you. Get some Rest". The note was clearly written by Christian. I wondered how he knew I would be arriving home late because *I* didn't know I would be arriving home late. I further wondered what made him decide on this evening to do such a kind gesture. I proceeded to ask him and he said, "This is for God". After hearing that statement, I perched my lips together and tilted my head in amazement. I quickly blew it off and proceeded to lay on the nicely "made up" couch. Christian cried out "NO! That's Not for You." He was very insistent that no one sit or lay on the couch and so no one did. His persistence had me very curious. What or *who* had he seen that I had not? What conversation had taken place between he and God? Christian would only answer so many questions and only *certain* questions before he completely refused to answer any more questions.

Now that I am older and my faith has grown more, I reflect back and wonder, have I made a comfortable place for God to enter? Have I opened my physical residence to Him?

Have I opened my heart for Him to make a permanent resting place for His Word and His Spirit?

Scripture:
Here I am! I stand at the door and knock. If anyone hears my voice and opens the door, I will come in and eat with that person, and they with me. Revelations 3:20 NIV

Reflection: When was the last time you made your dwelling open and comfortable for God to enter in? If you haven't done so recently, how will you now "make up" a place for Him?

_____

_____

_____

_____

_____

_____

Original poem written by Latressa A. Crawford.

I AM

I AM the one who really doesn't know where to begin.
It seems like that there is no beginning & I see no end.

I AM the one who is educated & smart
The one who crosses every I and dots every t
No I mean, dots every I and crosses every t.
Well… as you can see…
Can I be real & just be me??

Yes, I AM the one who is educated & smart
The one rooted in Christ & gives it her heart
But the one who seems to get hit by the darts.

I AM the daughter, the sister, the mother, Survivor
I AM the executive, preacher, minister, singer
I AM wifey, or soon to be, or playing like *I AM*
I AM the bread winner, the sole provider,
The one who brings home the bacon **and** the beef.

I AM the multitasker, the bill payer,
Ain't got no money so I gotta do my hair myself
Because I just used all my money on bills.

I AM the one who because she is strong
Gets passed over, even when she is crying out for help.

I AM the one who because she is Christ like
They try to shuck and jive.
Because **they** believe that Christ like means
Dumb, No Sense and Too Nice.

But…. Back up Boo I said, "CHRIST-LIKE"
The OLD ME AINT ALLL THE WAY DEAD

And with that begin said…

I AM the one who cries at night because her heart is heavy
I AM the one who just wants to be loved, who wants to be held.
Who wants to be told that she made them proud.

I AM the one who God wakes up even though she is hurting,
She intercedes for others.

I AM the one who God uses to build his Kingdom
Even when she is faced with adversities!

I AM the one who has demons to the left and demons to the right and even those demons have side demons who come at her.
Yet, Smiles and says *"How May I Serve Thee?"*…

I AM the one who is sick and tired of being sick and sick tired.
I AM the one who is TIRED of Saying she is Sick & Tired of being Sick & Tired of Being Sick & TIRED.

YES!

I AM weary, tired, burdened, feeling unloved, neglected, burnt out and feeling like I'm losing what I have

But…

***THE* I AM** comforts me
When I'm alone in my bed and have cried most of the night He whispers, *"Peace"*
And I fall off to sleep.

***THE* I AM** sends one of my number one oppressors
To assist and aide me.
He made them my footstool!

***THE* I AM** when I was quietly in need
Spoke to another on my behalf.
He provided for me.

***THE* I AM** when I was crying *out "WHAT IS WE GO DO?!?"*
Said, I Got You Boo..
No, FOR REAL… What Is We Go Do and How Is We Go Do It?!?
***THE* I AM** Said "I Got You. *I AM WHO, I AM*"
He provided a ram in the bush.

I AM….
***My* GOD!**

So, I guess I don't have to worry about the beginning or the end,
Because ***THE* I AM**, is the beginning and the end.

***THE* I AM** is my provider, my protector, my tear wiper, my comforter, my late night pillow talker.

THE **I AM** is resurrection & life.

Yes!

I AM the educator, executive, preacher, teacher, minister, wife, sister, mother, aunt, coworker, survivor, entrepreneur, artist, singer, praiser, worshipper…

AND because of *THE I AM…* **I AM able to be who I AM and MORE!!**

About the Author

Latressa A. Crawford is an educator, lifelong learner, writer, Kingdom builder and follower of Christ. Latressa is a mother of one son, Mr. Christian. It is her love for him that has led to the continuation of the outpour of love to others.

Originally from South Carolina, Latressa has spent half of her life in Charlotte, NC. While in Charlotte, her time was well spent serving in the community. Her involvement in the local and underserved community stems back to her younger years as she served alongside her mother, Dorinda Crawford, who was devoted to assisting those in need. In South Carolina, she has been featured on the local radio station (WLBG) expressing concerns and spreading awareness of community issues. These issues range from social awareness in the Black community and the plight of education. Also, Latressa was featured in the local newspaper (*Laurens Advertiser*) in SC for her planning and implementation of cultural awareness at the school where she taught. In addition, she and her class were chosen to be filmed on a segment of PBS for prototypical educational practices.

Latressa is presently continuing her educational practices as a servant leader with the underprivileged. She is ministry chair for ROH Reconnection Ministry, in which she collaborates with various agencies to service those in need. It is through this avenue that she goes into the streets and meets people where they are. She lends her services to other outside agencies (homeless shelters, women and children facilities, etc...) meeting the needs of God's people. Latressa has spoken and coordinated/taught Bible Studies at various churches in various states.

Latressa has made her mark as a noted writer. She has made writing contributions to various publications. She was a weekly contributor to STRUT! The Magazine and STRUT! The Magazine Online. In addition to that, her writings can be found in Trinette Collier's book "Sticky Notes" and Latressa is one of the coauthors of the book "STRUT: Another Collection of Words About Woman's Walk". *"Finding Joy in Everyday Life"* is her first published book which is intended to uplift and awaken the subconscious into finding the joy and the lesson/development in every situation that God chooses one to encounter.

A few of her acknowledgements include:
- 2014- STRUT Award, held in Atlanta.
- Teacher leader in the DeKalb County public system
- Christian Education Certification classes
- Recognition by the Georgia Department of Education for her exemplary examples of teaching state standards

Latressa A. Crawford......God's Chosen, a mother, friend, creative out of the box thinker, activist, encourager, public speaker, poet, author and more.

About the Contributor

Leah Campbell is a South Carolina native. As a graduate of Columbia College and the University of South Carolina, Leah has 19 years of experience as a Pediatric Speech Language Pathologist. She has worked in the hospital, school and clinical settings treating children with a variety of communication and developmental disorders.

Leah is married and the mother of two wonderful boys, ages 17 and 9. In her spare time, Leah enjoys traveling, reading and bowling.

Made in the USA
Columbia, SC
15 July 2024